Lingo Dingo
and the
Polish Chef

Written by Mark Pallis

Illustrated by James Cottell

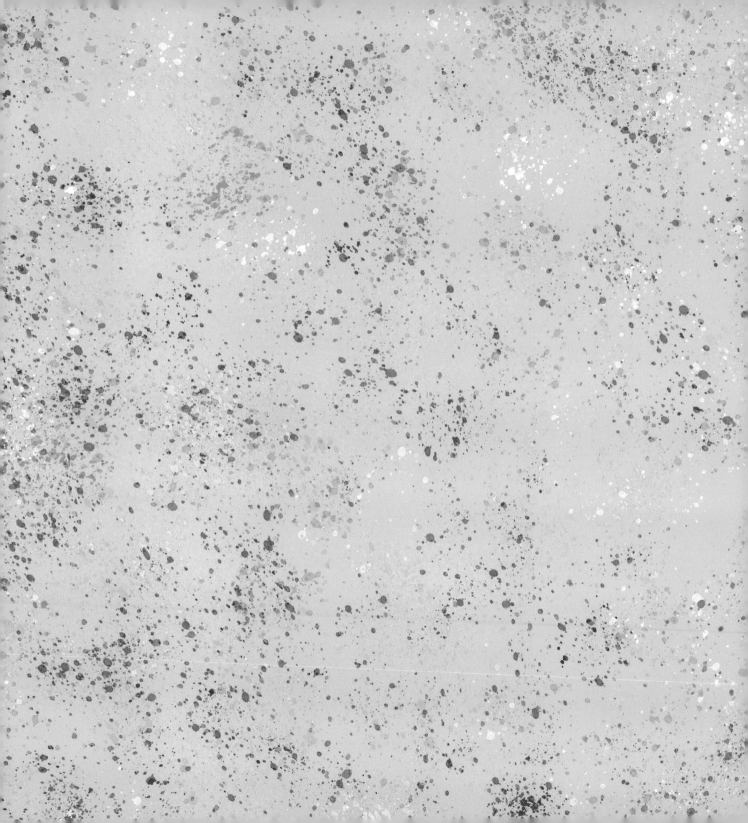

For my awesome sons Oscar and Felix - MP

For Leo and Juniper - JC

LINGO DINGO AND THE POLISH CHEF

Story edited by Natascha Biebow, Blue Elephant Storyshaping
First Printing, 2022
ISBN: 978-1-913595-94-4
NeuWestendPress.com

Lingo Dingo
and the
Polish Chef

Written by Mark Pallis

Illustrated by James Cottell

NEU WESTEND
— PRESS —

This is Lingo. She's a Dingo and she loves helping.
Anyone. Anytime. Anyhow.

Lingo often helps her stylish neighbour Gunther, who lives by himself next door. She does a few jobs and has a nice chat. It makes Gunter feel good and it makes Lingo feel good too.

One day, Lingo arranged a special birthday party for Gunther. She even ordered a cake from a famous Polish Chef.

There was a knock at the door, "It must be the cake!" said Lingo.
But it was a monkey.

"Witam. Jestem szefem kuchni Nono.
Mam problem," he said.

Oh no. I can't speak Polish yet, thought
Lingo. *Maybe 'Witam' is like 'Hello'.*

Witam = Hello; **Jestem** = My name is;
Mam problem = I have a problem

"Witam," said Lingo. Chef Nono replied slowly,
"Przykro mi, ale nie mogę upiec tortu urodzinowego."

"I don't understand," said Lingo. "But let me guess. You want..."

wózek = trolley; **ogórek kiszony** = gherkin;
balony = balloons; **nie** = no

"Mój piekarnik jest zepsuty," explained Chef.
"Mogę użyć twojego piekarnika?"

Chef's oven must be broken thought Lingo. "I know!
Let's bake the cake together," she said.

Mój piekarnik = my oven; **jest zepsuty** = is broken;
Mogę użyć twojego piekarnika? = can I use your oven?

Chef tapped his wrist. "Która jest godzina? Dziewiąta? Dziesiąta?" he asked.

Lingo showed Chef her watch.

"Jedenasta? Zaczynajmy! Szybko!"
They only had one hour until the party.

Chef Nono and Lingo whizzed around the kitchen:

Fartuch dla ciebie.

Trzepaczka.

Miska do mieszania.

fartuch = apron; **dla ciebie** = for you; **trzepaczka** = whisk
miska do mieszania = a mixing bowl

"Podaj mi proszę masło, cukier, jajka i mąkę," said Chef.

Lingo wasn't sure what those words meant, so she just grabbed fish, coffee and onions instead.

"Ryby, kawa i cebula. Obrzydliwe!" laughed Chef.

Podaj mi = pass me; masło = butter; cukier = sugar; jajka = eggs; i = and; mąkę = flour; proszę = please; ryby = fish; kawa = coffee; cebula = onions; obrzydliwe = disgusting

Chef plopped butter, sugar, eggs and flour into a bowl. "So that's what 'masło, cukier, jajka i mąka' means!" laughed Lingo.

"Ja mieszam, ty mieszasz, my mieszamy," said Chef and together they began to mix the cake.

ja mieszam = I mix; **ty mieszasz** = you mix; **my mieszamy** = we mix

"Na koniec, proszek do pieczenia. Dwie łyżeczki," said Chef. Lingo guessed 'proszek do pieczenia' meant baking powder, but how much?

Before she could ask, Chef hurried away, saying,
"Przepraszam, muszę zrobić siusiu."

Lingo laughed, "I can guess what 'siusiu' means!"

Na koniec = finally; **proszek do pieczenia** = baking powder; **dwie** = two;
łyżeczki = spoonfulls; **przepraszam** = excuse me; **muszę zrobić siusiu** = I need to do a wee wee

I wonder if this is too much? thought Lingo as she added ten spoonfulls of 'proszek do pieczenia' to the mix.

She carefully put everything into the oven and before long, a sweet cakey smell filled the kitchen.

proszek do pieczenia = baking powder

"Co się stało? To jest ogromne!" said Chef.

Lingo realised she had added too much baking powder.

"Sorry," she said sheepishly.

They somehow got the cake out of the oven but ...

it was so big ...

... they couldn't hold it. "Disaster!" cried Lingo. "Katastrofa!" wailed Chef.

Katastrofa = disaster

"I know what will make you feel better," said Lingo, kindly. 'Eat this 'Ogórek kiszony'!"

"Obrzydliwe. Nienawidzę ogórków." said Chef.

They were running out of time.

ogórków = gherkins; **obrzydliwe** = disgusting; **nienawidzę** = I hate

"I've got it! Gunther loves hats, so let's turn the cakey mess into a hat cake! " said Lingo.

First she shaped the cake, then she filled balloons with icing.

Next came the best part: POP! POP! POP!

It was a messy job but in the end, the cake looked fantastic. "Czerwony, pomarańczowy, żółty, zielony, niebieski. Fantastycznie!" said Chef.

czerwony = red; pomarańczowy = orange; żółty = yellow;
zielony = green; niebieski = blue; fantastycznie = fantastic

There was a knock at the door.
"Drzwi!" said Chef.
It was Gunther, and he was
wearing his special hat!

"Thank you. This makes me
feel so special," said Gunther.
"You are special," replied Lingo.

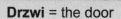

Drzwi = the door

Gunter was thrilled with his cake.

Chef's deep voice sang "Sto lat, sto lat. Niech żyje, żyje nam."

Sto lat, sto lat, niech żyje, żyje nam = 100 years, 100 years, may they live (Polish happy birthday song)

"Dmuchnij!" said Chef.

Gunther blew out all the candles in one puff and everyone tucked in.

dmuchnij = blow

"Ja jem, ty jesz, on je, ona je, oni jedzą," laughed Chef. "Jemy!" added Lingo proudly.

ja jem = I eat; **ty jesz** = you eat; **on je** = he eats;
ona je = she eats; **oni jedzą** = they eat; **jemy** = we eat

The friends watched the sun as it set in the sky.

"Ja jestem szczęśliwy,
ty jesteś szczęśliwy,
wszyscy jesteśmy szczęśliwi! cheered Chef

---

ja jestem szczęśliwy = I am happy; **ty jesteś szczęśliwy** = you are happy;
wszyscy jesteśmy szczęśliwi! = everyone is happy;

Baking a cake, helping a friend, learning a new language... what a day!

But now it was time for bed. It was time to dream about all the fun things that might happen tomorrow.

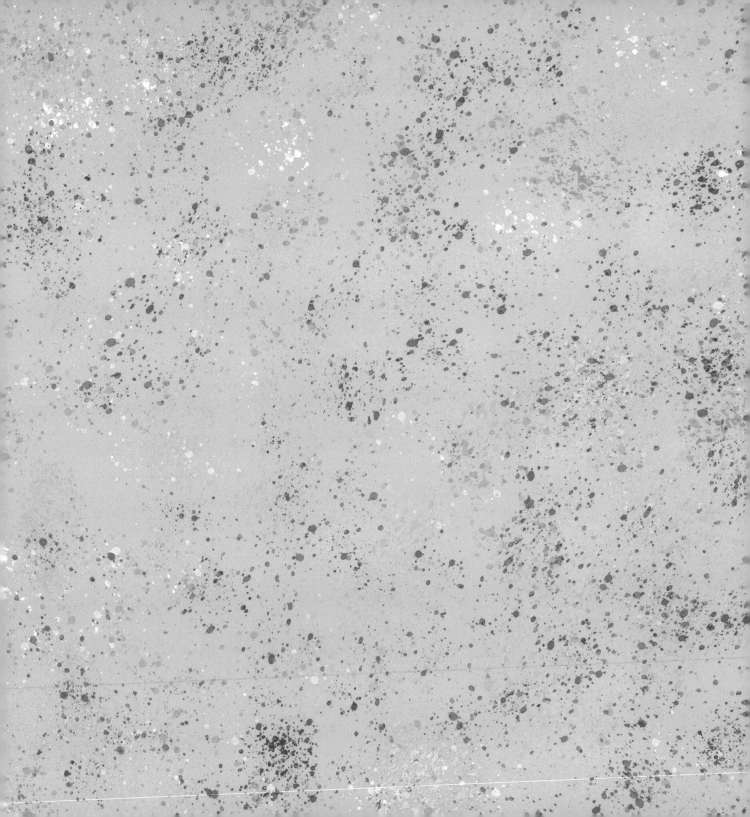

Learning to love languages

An additional language opens a child's mind, broadens their horizons and enriches their emotional life. Research has shown that the time between a child's birth and their sixth or seventh birthday is a "golden period" when they are most receptive to new languages. This is because they have an in-built ability to distinguish the sounds they hear and make sense of them. The Story-powered Language Learning Method taps into these natural abilities.

How the Story-powered language learning Method works

We create an emotionally engaging and funny story for children and adults to enjoy together, just like any other picture book. Studies show that social interaction, like enjoying a book together, is critical in language learning.

Through the story, we introduce a relatable character who speaks only in the new language. This helps build empathy and a positive attitude towards people who speak different languages. These are both important aspects in laying the foundations for lasting language acquisition in a child's life.

As the story progresses, the child naturally works with the characters to discover the meanings of a wide range of fun new words. Strategic use of humour ensures that this subconscious learning is rewarded with laughter; the child feels good and the first seeds of a lifelong love of languages are sown.

For more information and free learning resources visit www.neuwestendpress.com

You can learn more words and phrases with these hilarious, heartwarming stories from NEU WESTEND PRESS

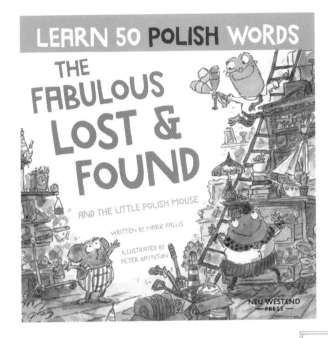

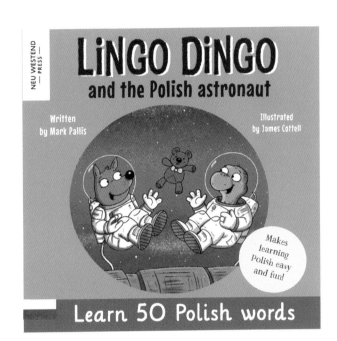

"...nt people to be so busy laughing,
they don't realise they're learning!"
Mark Pallis

Crab and Whale is the bestselling story of how a little Crab helps a big Whale. It's carefully designed to help even the most energetic children find a moment of calm and focus. It also includes a special mindful breathing exercise and affirmation for children.
Also available in French, Italian, German & Spanish!
Featured as one of Mindful.org's
'Seven Mindful Children's books'

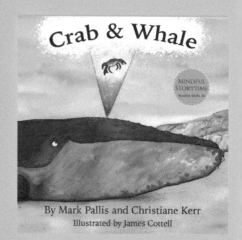

Do you call them hugs or cuddles?

In this funny, heartwarming story, you will laugh out loud as two loveable gibbons try to figure out if a hug is better than a cuddle and, in the process, learn how to get along.

A perfect story for anyone who loves a hug (or a cuddle!)

www.markpallis.com

Printed in Great Britain
by Amazon

80458991R00022